Hesitant to Start

and other poems

Robert D. Williams

DEDICATION

W. O. McCabe

Beloved Grandfather, friend

and storyteller at heart.

CONTENTS

CONTENTS

CONTENTS

ACKNOWLEDGMENTS

When you finish a project there is that lag time before you work up the energy and/or nerve before starting a new one. There is that lingering doubt if it will get finished and will it be good enough. Fortunately, I have a good support group to encourage me to write and oddly enough read my efforts. I particularly want to thank Sue Casey, Cindy Casey, Ruth Gnagi, Cathy Casey Hoffman, Trina Lee, Woody Gimbel, and Shelly Mason who have read my lines more than once and made excellent suggestion. I also want to acknowledge the tremendous support and thoughtful comments of the members of the Writer's Corner, at the Healthy Living Center, and the Windmill Poets. These individuals provide the needed motivation to write daily and try to match the excellent work they share. I also want to thank Scott, Pat S., Ali, David, Joy, Margaret, Kathy, Billy, Dave, Kelly, Kevin, Cornelius, Jim, the two Taylors, Ashli, B'journ and numerous others at BJ's and Interurban for the gentle teasing and useful conversations. A special thanks to my wife Pat and daughters Sarah and Ann, without them there would be no words. Finally, a sincere thank you to the managers, bar tenders, waiters, cooks, and helpers at the Interurban on Memorial where I spent many quiet hours writing in my journal and wrote many of the poems for "Sitting at the Bar." Unfortunately, it closed its doors on Sunday, September 20, 2020, and like the loss of a close friend, it and they will be sorely missed.

Hesitant to Start

Well-Chosen Words, Well-Turned Phrase

Pen poised above the paper,
but I fail to make a mark.
Hesitant to start.
Yes, I've done this before,
but can I do it again?

Can I choose the right words
to convey the scene, or memory, or thought
that's in my mind or heart to paper?
Make you see, or feel, or hear
what I intend? If I'm successful
will I pull at your heart strings?
Make you feel sad, thoughtful,
angry, or indifferent?

Will you hear the child's laughter?
See the light dance between two lovers' eyes?
Or the solitude and loneliness
of the person sitting at the end of the bar?
Hear the whisper of the wind in the trees,
or the call of the lone cicada?
Feel the sun's warmth on a cold day,
or watch the night's sky change colors at dawn?
Read the grief in an elder's face
written by the lines etched there?

Yes, there is an inkling of failure here.
And even when I finish there is always doubt.

Self-Doubt

Desire urges me on, while fear bridals me.
Giordano Bruno

We all have it –
at least to some extent.
Even when we've done it before,
whatever "it" is,
there is that lingering fear,
can I do it again?

Will it be as good –
as before?
Can I finish it?
Should I finish it?
Can't you do better –
my father's voice inside my head.

Ignore the voices.
Follow desire and passion.
Use the doubt to push you forward.
Besides without doubt – would we grow?
Where would the challenge be?

String Theory

Do you feel unraveled?
That in your knit one, purl two
you've dropped a stitch?
That your weft has left its warp?

Do you feel that your thoughts are uncollected?
Lines, tangled and broken, frayed at the ends?
Partial conversations and phrases drag
behind you, like the chains on Marley's ghost?
That to gather them up you might try
crochet or macramé?
But you don't know a slip- from a square-knot.

Knock your loom aright.
Grab that last line floating by
and like a Navajo weaver
start at the bottom and weave to the top.

Lines

have you written lines
that blur your vision
or make you cry

magic vowels
and unique phrases
that take you to another place

where time stands still –
what a moment that is
and all too brief

Untitled Verses 1 to 3

1. Magnolia blossoms
   freshly white
   on a sea of green

2. Flashes of blue and white
   clear song in the air
   Blue Jay at the feeder

3. Thin threads float on the wind
   sparkle in the sunlight
   spider migration

Sitting at the Bar

Paddi's Lament

So, there I was, the night pitch black,
sitting on the stonewall surrounding the cemetery.
I had meant to go earlier but stopped by the pub
and raised a few with the boys.
Well, you know how that goes.

It was St. Paddi's Day you see
and I was going to pay my respect to ol'Mick.
My best mate. God rest his rotten soul.

I had a bottle of the finest with me
to share with him a drink or two.
One little nip to settle my nerves,
I dropped down to the ground below.

It was quiet. It was eerie.
I took another swallow for my nerves
and began to search for his grave.

As I said it was a dark night, strange it was.
I stumbled around for a while,
and took another drink or three,
when I saw a greenish light just ahead.

And damn if it weren't ol'Mick's grave all a glow,
and a wee elf sitting on his head stone,
giving off a humming sound.

Well, scared like, I took another sip.
I stared at her and rubbed my eyes,
and blinked, but she didn't disappear.

Green she was in body and dress.
Even her hair was green – each braid a different hue.
She just sat there looking at me with bright green eyes,

and when her dragonfly wings stopped
the humming died away and greenish glow dimmed.

I blinked again wishing she would go as well.
Most of the little people I see do.
But she didn't and said in a sweet little voice
"You're late. Where have you been?"
in an accusing tone similar to my ol'lady's.

Well, tis dark, and scary, and I got lost you see.
Went to all this trouble bring him a drink.
Couldn't find his grave, I said.

So, I opened the bottle, turned it over,
and nary a drop hit the ground.

"I told Mick that you never get here with it —
as much as Mick misses his drink.
I said the temptation, the thirst, be too much for you.
But he said, "Paddï just might. Just for once in his life."
Mick was certain, so certain,
I said if you did, three wishes I would give.
Too bad. So sad." And with that she flitted away.

Damn! One swallow would have been enough.
I dropped the bottle and fell to my knees,
and cried and bawled like I never.
Tears as green as emeralds they were
and where they dropped on the ground
shamrocks sprouted and grew.
I slept where I wept.

When morning came, I found meself in a lush bed
of shamrocks that covered Mick's grave and
clear headed like I've never been the day after.
Was it all a dream? The elf in green? The three wishes?
Or was it all Mick and one of his damn silly jokes?

Well enough said about that.
Me glass is empty.
Get me another

Elfin Server

Her elfin, lithe body
danced among the tables
serving food and beverage
as an art form like no other.

Country Music

Sitting at the bar
listening to country music
and muted conversations.
Thinking about the days behind,
as well as the days ahead.
No, I'm not counting either –
regretting one or anticipating the other.
Mainly reflecting on how things have changed –
wondering what changes are to come.

Slippage

The loose-fitting long-sleeved tee-shirt
slid to the edge of her shoulder
as she leaned forward to talk with her friend.

As their meal continued more tanned skin became visible
with each movement and gesture.
Soon the top of her arm
and a flesh colored bra strap appeared.

It was more amusing than inviting
as the slow downward slippage progressed.
Would there possibly be a glimpse of a breast?
Or would she finally realize the fact
and put an end to the act?

The Spider and the Fly

With apologies to Mary Howitt.

The fly stood at the threshold
looking at the sign above the door.
A pen and ink drawing of a dragon
flying above the sea.

Below the dragon a warning –
"Beyond here dragons be."
And below that in a small hand,
"Enter and let your imagination reign."

"Come in. Come in," the spider beckoned.
"You'll be quite safe.
It's late in the day. I've already ate."
The fly hesitated.

"No. No. Seriously come in.
I assure you; you will come to no harm.
Come in and sit a spell. Let us talk.
And then I'll spin a yarn."

"For in here I am a teller of tales,
and a writer of lines.
I let my mind wander,
and think of all kinds of things."

"So, come in and be at ease.
This is a very comfortable chair.
A brandy? A glass of wine?
I'm having port myself. A cigar, maybe?"

"Yes. Pleasant here among my books
and writings. A lovely day today.
I think I will tell you a story.
You'll be the hero and daring deeds you'll do."

"Maybe you'll slay a dragon
and save a damsel or two.
Such adventures we will have –
the story we will spin together."

"And if we should die tomorrow
it will matter not.
For in the lines of the story,
we will always be."

Confusion or Illusion

I tried to read a poem.
Actually, I read it twice.
None of it made sense.

It was in a language I understood.
At least it seemed so.
I knew the words.

I didn't need the unabridged dictionary.
Nor did I Google any phrase.
But still the meaning of the poem escaped me.

The form was odd –
lines broke across the page.
At first, I thought it was two separate poems.

But no matter how hard I tried
the point eluded me.
It reminded me of Freshman Comp.

Beat poetry was all the rage.
Those verses were jarring and elusive as well.
The meanings hidden among the lines.

Like I was sitting in a smoke-filled room,
drinking coffee, and smoking unfiltered cigarettes,
snapping my fingers and saying "Cool man!"

I enjoy reading poetry and it needn't rhyme,
or be written by Frost, or Auden, or Old William himself,
but I like to come away with something to think about.

Now don't get me wrong I like a challenge,
but this poem appeared to be a joke.
Really, does anyone understand it?

Did the reviewers and editor of the journal?
Or did they read it and scratch their heads,
snap their fingers and say "Cool man!"

Young Love

Across the way a young couple slid
into a booth and leaned across the table
to hold each other's hands.

I couldn't see her face,
but his was plainly seen;
smiles playing on his lips and in his eyes.

They parted long enough to order,
then held hands again.
Her thumb rubbed the back of his hand.

Were his eyes dilated?
Did his heart skip a beat?
Did he even taste what he ate? Did she?

They left holding hands.
Bless them in their youth.
Will they make it? We can only hope.

Were we ever that young, all those years ago?
Did we know any more than they,
or did we just think we did?

Untitled Verses 4 to 7

4. as clouds floated in the sky
   their shadows danced across the fields
   playing tag from hilltop to hilltop

5. the sharp turn – the face – her eyes
   he had stepped into a mine field
   his mind raced to tip-toe out

6. red flashes against green leaves
   his mate on the ground
   eats seed fallen from the feeder

7. muffled sounds of thunder
   timpani of raindrops
   memories wash away

In Search of Wisdom

Wisdom

In the forest of the night
sitting in a small clearing
on the trunk of an ancient tree,
fallen long ago.

The bright moon casts shadows
deep and dark in the woods
that surrounds me.
An owl calls. I answer.

On quiet wing it lands next to me.
Turning its head, it looks at me,
and throughout the night
we exchange memories
without word or touch.

As dawn breaks, the owl
shakes its feathers
and on swift and silent wings
leaves as soundlessly as it came.

I sat longer in that quiet
and forgotten place in time,
to ponder the mysteries instilled.

Sophia

From an early age I've searched for you.
I found your sisters Prudence and Patience.
But you always slipped away.

Chasing shadows would be easier.
Longing for you, I read the Sages' works.
They valued your gift above gold or silver.

Yet you give it willingly to those who seek it.
And still my search continues.
Others of your kind I've found.

Learned from them and gained knowledge.
My search has taken many paths.
Insight provides a glimpse of you.

But how does one know
what Wisdom is?
Would I even know you when we finally meet?

Vessel of Memories

He who cannot draw on three thousand years is living from hand to mouth.
                                                            Goethe

As the elders gathered around the counsel fire
a young girl sat in the shadows,
listened to their stories,
the history of her people.
Remembered the discussions
and the solutions to problems.
And as the elders came and went
she sat quietly absorbing all she heard.

When she was older, she took her place
among the elders, remained still
and listened while the others talked.
During a heated discussion the others grew silent,
turned to her and waited …

In a soft voice she spoke:

"As a young girl something similar happened.
This is what was said. This is what was done."

When did we lose the ability
to sit quietly, to listen, and think?
To hear our stories and learn from them?
When did we fail to gain Wisdom?

Reflection

I.

Standing in the doorway
watching the snow fall,
I'm reminded that no two snowflakes
are quite the same.

II.

Snowflakes fall to the earth,
covering all in a soft white blanket.
Quiet ensues, as the snow muffles sound,
and peace covers the land.

Is this Nature's way to remind us
to pause, reflect and meditate?
A quiet time to listen to our own thoughts,
or hear the voice of another?

III.

Meditation is a doorway
leading to knowledge and insight,
reminding us, as the snowflakes do,
we are more alike than different.

Interlude

The clock struck the first note of the hour,
hesitated and struck the next.
In that instant, time seemed to stand still –
an eerie quiet filled the house.

I waited for the next strike,
wishing it would come and break the silence.
As if holding my breath
could will time to move.

Does time stop between the strikes of the clock?
Or the ticks of the minute hand?
The beats of your heart?
Or the thoughts that you think?

Solitude

Heard melodies are sweet, but those unheard are sweeter.
                                        Keats

Early morning in a dark house
I sit near a window, drink my tea
and listen to the quiet.

I hear the sound of my breathing
and feel the heart thumping in my chest.
The silence punctuated by the clock's ticking.

The mantel clock in the upstairs study
chimes the half-hour,
answered by the clock in the den.

As the sky lightens, birds begin to sing,
the wind sighs through the tree branches,
and windchimes play a soft melody.

Yet the house is still asleep,
the world outside is barely stirring –
solitude surrounds me.

My mind is free to roam that empty realm,
diving into the benevolent and peaceful depth
where I hear the sounds unheard.

Listening

Humanity's problem stems from the inability
to sit in a quiet room alone.

Blaise Pascal

Why is it that our world has to be filled with sound and motion?
Must we always have radio or television or YouTube –
to occupy our time?
Is it possible to spend 10 minutes without checking
our cell phones or devices?

The more technology surrounds us
the more separated we become from
from the voice within.

Find a calm place, be it outside or within,
and sit quietly listening to the sounds around you:
the song of a bird, the rustle of leaves in the wind,
the ticking of a clock, the hum of the fan blades,
the soft purr of a cat.

Empty your thoughts and listen quietly
for the voice you hear is the one you answer to.

Pursuit

As a young man he desperately
pursued happiness
only to discover
as an old man
happiness surrounded him
if he stood still.

The Leaf

For the longest time
watching a leaf
just one among the many
twisting and turning
fluttering in the wind
a thought came to me.
Is the leaf playing in the wind,
or is the wind playing with the leaf?
It is a matter of perspective.
Which do you choose?

Man in the Mirror

I'm starting with the man in the mirror
I'm asking him to change his ways
                          Siedah Garrett / Glen Ballard

This morning I stood in front of the mirror
washing my face – thinking of the day.
Remembered that the distance
between the image and the mirror's surface
is equal to the distance
between me and the mirror.

What lies in that seemingly dimensionless space
between the image and the mirror's surface?
Is it the potential of the day?
The multi-dimensional space I'll travel
with each decision I make
as I make my way through the day?

Who will I be?
Will I remember to tell my wife I love her?
Feel the love of family –
or the warmth of friends?

Be kind and generous –
or impatient and ill tempered?
Reflective and thankful for my blessings –
or overly anxious about the things I can't control.

So many paths throughout the day
on each decision hangs,
one of multiple futures.
So many different selves I could be.

All that potential behind the mirror
or is all that potential in the image –
that's me.

Untitled Verses 8 to 10

8. Bordered by green ribbons
    the road stretched into the distance
    pressed against the earth by dark gray clouds.

9. The rusted roof's subtle slide to the ground
    chronicles the barn's decay
    like clock hands mark the passing hours.

10. Standing on the caprock
    watching a storm in the distance.
    Dark clouds move quickly across the mesa –
    lightning strikes a tree across the road.

Scatter My Ashes

Prairie Sky

On a moonless winter's night
standing in a pasture
far from city lights and sounds
I took in the night sky.

Blue-black with a myriad of stars,
the Milky Way stretched across the heavens,
looked like a cathedral ceiling decorated
with a mosaic of brilliant glass tiles.

I stood in the complete silence.
Only the wind's soft whisper
and the distant call of a lone coyote
penetrated the wonder that embraced me.

Scatter My Ashes

No cemetery plot,
no granite headstone,
no pine box or cement vault.
Just scatter my ashes
and call it done.

Find a two-lane road in the country,
long and empty except for fields
and fence lines, trees and brush,
where my ashes,
and those of my dogs,
can be scattered along the roadside
among the grasses and wild flowers.

Don't mark the area.
No need to return.
Just think of me and my dogs
warmed by the sun,
wetted by rain,
hearing the wind sing through blades of grass,
watching the wonders of the prairie night sky;
the endless walks the dogs and I
will have watching the seasons change.

Millie

I know you still look for me;
see me out of the corner of your eye.
Hear me walk across the floor,
or climb the stairs.
Do you wake and listen for me,
and then realize I'm no longer there?
I admit I miss hearing you talk
and sitting under the arbor,
watching the birds.
Being the first to hear the lines
you just finished.
Your understanding of my needs,
without a word spoken.
It was not an easy decision, my leaving.
No, not easy for either of us,
but it had to come.
I will wait for you next to the others.
But think of us how we were;
not as ashes in boxes on the shelf.
Someday we will all be scattered together
along a roadside or across a field,
to watch the moon and sun rise and set;
the changing of the seasons –
and be a part of creation.

Hannah

A soft growl floated up
from the old Basset hound
sleeping quietly on the floor
next to me.

Her body still,
but her facial muscles twitched.
Nose quivered. Lips flexed.
Eye brows arched. Ears perked.

Sound asleep. Yet her mind active.
What does she dream about?
Does she dream about her sister?
Are memories of her still there?

Millie passed a year ago this month.
A hot July like this one. No warning.
The cancer quietly doing its work.
Healthy one day. The next day not.

The loss of her sister changed Hannah.
She stays closer to my wife and me.
For several weeks she whined
at the backdoor until I returned.

Was she waiting for me to bring Millie home?
When did she realize that she was alone?
It was a month or more before Hannah
moved in to a routine of "just her."

Some days while I watch Hannah in the yard,
I look for Millie. Still odd not seeing them both.
I wonder if Hannah remembers –
does she miss her – as I do.

Untitled Verses 11 to 13

11. The wind rippled the lake's surface,
    as the hawk swooped earthward,
    pulling up at the last minute –
    cry of frustration.

12. The old barn sat across the lake
    on a grassy knoll.
    Its fellows less fortunate,
    lay deep beneath the water's surface –
    homes for fishes.

13. Sitting on the porch, looking at the lake
    a cardinal calls from a nearby tree.
    Each call, unanswered, perked up the cat's ears –
    a slight smile on its face.

When the Darkness Lingers

Blind Alley, Darkened Recesses

Habituée of darkness I have become.
John Montague

In a wakeful dream
I walk down a dark alley
like a character in a noir picture.
Unlike the film, sounds of footsteps
do not follow.

Nor is there the scurrying of rats,
the cry of a cat,
bottles breaking,
or the slamming of a door.

No, this silent alley of crumbled buildings
is in the darkened recesses of my memory.
Behind these boarded windows and doors
unwanted memories reside.

Murder, mayhem or stolen goods?
No, these are memories
of embarrassment and regret.
A sharply spoken word or action.
Or worse – an unspoken word and inaction.

Memories that when recalled – fester.
Like picking a scab until it bleeds,
and again, feel the guilt, or the shame,
as you once did.

Maybe if there were a menacing presence
hiding in a darkened door way,
the area strewn with garbage,
and the lingering smell of decay,
my thoughts would not venture here.

All I know is with my last breath
these buildings will crumble to dust.
I will be free of these memories,
and they will be free of me.

Golden Yesterdays

Say goodbye to golden yesterdays
or your heart will never enjoy to love the present.
Anthony de Mello, SJ

The lines above reminded me of my mother.
Even when she was young, she preferred to tell
and retell stories of her past.
The places she and my father lived, the people they knew,
stories of my sister and me growing up.
Good times and sad times.

As she grew older, I think she preferred the past to the present.
She lived in the present. Her mind was sharp.
But when we visited, we would slip into the old stories –
retold, again and again.

Sequestered in place by the Pandemic of 2020,
with the normal schedule of our lives disrupted,
the loss of contact with family, friends, writers,
and people at the grocery and elsewhere
has made me feel older than I am.

Now my thoughts seem to slip too easily into the past.
The good times and bad. The struggles.
The victories. The loss of grandparents and parents.
 Passing of friends and close, and not-so-close, colleagues.
The warmth of the house filled with family.

When I find I am wandering too far down that road,
I remind myself that the potential of all tomorrows
are the new memories for the coming yesterdays.

Thumb Up, Thumb Down

It happens with such regularity
we should be accustomed to it.
The viral photo, video or quote.
Is it true?
Don't bother with such mundane things.
React immediately, don't think –
vent your anger.

When I see this,
I often think of an old movie.
A medieval town,
angry villagers with flaming torches;
wielding axe handles and pitchforks.
The inflamed mob, looking for a scapegoat,
pulls an old woman from her hovel,
and burns her at the stake.
Good. That's done.
Things will be better now.

Or maybe you would appreciate
a more modern version.
The mob storms the jail,
grabs the prisoner,
drags him through town,
and hangs him.
Is this person guilty?
Does it matter?

Or maybe we should
get together and stone them.
Here, take this rock.
Of course, *you* wouldn't do *that*.

Social media is today's pillory.
So, before you add your comment,
forward the message, or twit your tweet,
imagine yourself as Nero
watching the bloody carnage –
will you take part?
Thumb up or thumb down?

Time: A Golden Wind

Time's but a golden wind that shakes the grass.
Siegfried Sassoon

Reading a poem written about WWI,
a single line stopped me.
Made me think –
how full of meaning one line can be.

The men in the trenches
didn't know when the next shell would fall,
or when a sniper's bullet would find its mark.
They lived from minute to minute.

Each minute precious and too short.
Yet, some seemed to last a lifetime.
Life tucked away –
between moments of pure joy and sheer horror.

Like the breeze that moves a blade of grass
life passes by too quickly –
then all is shadow.

Belladonna

I saw her in the garden
just as evening gathered –
drawn to her slim figure
and her elegant grace.

Nearing her, fragrance assaulted my senses,
giddiness and shortness of breath.
I felt her drawing me closer –
there was no escape.

I felt a flush of blinding passion,
that set my heart to race.
Only her possession would
diminish my overwhelming desire.

Sensuous hands reached out to me,
fingers interlaced with mine,
held me as close as tendrils
that support a climbing vine.

As suddenly as passion possessed me
coldness filled me with dread.
With a final seizure,
she left me for dead.

Trend of the Day

Trend of the day –
would sound so much better in French.
Or maybe as a Latin phrase, as

Carpe diem
or
Illegitimus non carborundum est

which really isn't Latin.

But the trend is so apparent,
at least to me, you will understand
without such embellishments.

Basically, we have become
a nation of apologists.
Hardly a day goes by that someone
isn't apologizing for something they've done,
said or written, recently or
in the past, that now is deemed offensive.

Worse they are apologizing for family
members or others for transgressions
in the past now considered wrong by today's standards.
Is there no statute of limitations?

My great grandfather Williams emigrated
from Germany and entered the US via Texas.
(Too many Jews in New York
so, they were shunted to elsewhere.)
His wife and her family had been here for some time.
My mother's family goes back to the earliest landings.

Through the generations my ancestors have helped
establish this country and its promise using
principles appropriate and honorable of the times.
Should I judge them by today's standards?

Should I find fault with those that fought
in the French and Indian War, the Revolutionary War,
The War of 1812, Civil War (on both sides), WWI, or WWII?

Should I fault those that might have owned slaves?
Or the ones I know came over as indentured servants?
Where do we draw the line?

I know I have told sexist, even racist,
jokes in my past. Jokes I wouldn't tell today.
Yes, I've learned. Matured with age. Most do.

Should we then call out someone that wrote
a paper in their youth years later to apologize?
Or should we determine what the person stands for now
and make our determination based on that?

How many generations do the sins of the fathers go back?
It probably won't matter in the long run.
We will have devoured ourselves in an orgy
of apologies and self-flagellation by then.

Memory: Prison or Trap

….. memory is a poor man's prison.
                    Christian Wiman

Why is memory a poor man's prison?
I didn't find the answer in the poem.
Yet, I couldn't stop thinking about the line –
maybe that was the point.

Sometimes I think of memory as a necessary evil.
Required for thought, reasoning,
judgment, empathy, love.
Without it we couldn't learn from our mistakes;
there would be no development.

But memories can be elusive and beguiling.
They are shapeshifters of the mind,
recalling events that might have happened,
or modified by time so the truth is obscured.

Memories can be more comforting, reassuring
than the reality in which we live.
Thus, ensnaring us to live in the past
instead of living in the present.

Memories have a menacing aspect as well.
Drawing on them we can obsess on past mistakes,
unkindnesses, hurt feelings, perceived wrongs,
and there is the waiting trap.

Drifting

I sometimes feel I am drifting through life;
making the motions,
succeeding when necessary,
but not really connected,
not totally engaged.

An actor playing a role,
pretending to be what I am,
or what people expect,
a caricature based on imaginings,
but not what I am.

Pretender maybe,
playing at work, family and life;
successes achieved, not really earned,
rather an award for playing pretend,
and not getting caught.

Does everyone feel this way at times?
Do we all wonder what we are doing -
      or why?
Are we successful, or just think we are?
But the nagging question is:

Am I as smart as I think I am,
or as I pretend?

Last Breath

"Come, let me kiss you with my dying breath,
that my soul might linger."

Such an odd line to come to me,
especially in mid-afternoon on a sunny day.
This is a line that should come in the early morning hours,
in the quiet; in the dark.

Have I read this somewhere?
Is it some deep memory, or an original thought?
Honestly, I couldn't decide as I pondered it.

Is it uttered by a lover leaving their loved one?
Who would think of their last breath,
or want their soul to linger?

Would a kiss impart their breath,
their spirit, their soul –
would the soul linger?

If it did linger would it be a blessing,
or a curse?

The Tower

I am in a cell of my own making.
At the bottom of a tall crumbling tower
of large granite stones, sitting on a lonely knoll.

I've fallen deeper this time.
The top of the tower seems farther away,
and the pinhole of light above my head
barely penetrates the Stygian gloom.

A darkness so thick no sounds echo,
a damp chill no warmth can drive away;
depression so deep it crushes your spirit.

I know every inch of my cell by memory.
Every crack in the wall, the worn stone steps
spiraling to the top mimicking my plunge to its depth.

Yes, I've been here before,
many times, but never this deep – this long.
But why I am here is a mystery,
the usual triggers were not there.

Is it the semi-isolation due to the pandemic?
The disruption of our schedules?
Loss of contact with friends and family?
Or is it the uncertainty of what will be next?

Who would have guessed the chaos the year has brought?
Protests, riots, upheaval and indecision,
vitriol and hatred spewed on television and social media.
The maddening pace to throw out the old,
but no clue as what to replace the "old" with.

Everyone thinks it will get better after November,
after the political debates and election,
and the arrival of a vaccine. But I think not.
The trend is set.

Maybe, I am better off where I am. No –
No, I'll slowly crawl up the stairs, pretend I'm better;
try to be optimistic though I'm not.

Untitled Verses 14 and 15

14. Through winter's gray clouds
    a glimpse of the sun
    that neither warms,
    nor gladdens the heart.

15. Gray sky brightens,
    but the light casts no shadows.
    Sorrow creeps into the heart,
    but need not stay there.

Moments Remembered

Symphony of Letters

In the quiet of the morning,
I hear the pen move across my journal.
Each swirl, dash, dot, or letter –
a note upon the page.

Letters to words. Words to phrase.
Thoughts flow over the page.
An orchestration of mind, body, and pen.
Each word flowing from the pen's tip.
Some words finish before thought is complete –
magical moments, filled with the pen's music.

My grandchildren will never hear
this music, or see this magic.
They didn't learn cursive writing,
nor can they easily read it.
Printing is sufficient. Digital is the way.

So, these lines I write this morning
may not be a symphony of letters,
but a dirge for the written word.

Pale Blue Sky, Pale Blue Sea

Looking at the pale blue sky, took me back –
standing on a cliff above the ocean,
blue waters below and blue sky above,
as a coffin was slowly lowered into the ground.

Standing by my father at the military cemetery,
we watch a Chief's son laid to rest.
Later, his father would be interred with him.
They would rest together
until the klaxon sounds a call to stations,
or an angelic horn announces reveille.

My high school friend stood with us.
For over a year we had watched
his younger brother waste away,
looking more like a death-camp survivor
than a young teenager.
My first experience with cancer,
and with death.

It hadn't been all bad.
There were good days talking with him,
sharing his love of reading,
watching the fish in his saltwater aquarium,
remembering his love of all things aquatic,
or sneaking him out the window
to go fishing at a neighbor's pond.
His laughter as his mother pulled our ears
when we returned.

My vision of that day,
standing above the ocean
and his last days in bed came unbidden,
blurred by watery eyes,
all due to a pale blue sky.

Magical Moment

Lit a match
watched the dancing flame
the ribbon of smoke in the air.

What draws us to a flame
the glow of a candle
the warmth of a fire?

Some primitive memory of early man
taming of fire to light the darkness
shadows dancing on the cavern wall?

The smallness of a flame
or the power within.

Steps

Looking up from my reading
I watched Pat walk through
the door into the kitchen.

How many times have I watched
her enter or leave a room
during our 50 plus years of marriage?

Go out the door to work,
shop, volunteer, or meet a friend,
with a little twinge of expectation
of her return.

That same twinge I felt
numerous times sitting by
her hospital bed.

Like stepping from this room
to that room –
but with no return.

How do you measure a life with someone?
Step by step, moment by moment?
By the minute, or hour, or day, or week?

Years that seem to slip by too quickly?
I try to settle these thoughts as I listen
to her make her tea; toast her English muffin.

Just trying to take this moment in,
savoring it for what it is …
a gift, and a blessing.

Ode To A Rocker

I didn't place you by the trash bins.
Nor did I set you on the curb to be hauled away.
If it had been left to me –
you would still be under the arbor.

How many years were we together?
Was it my 40th birthday when the girls bought you?
So, it's been 30 years, or more –
it doesn't seem that long.

For the majority of those years
you sat in my office.
How many papers and books did we read?
And the number of manuscripts we wrote,
or reviewed for journals?

How many visitors sat and rocked?
Those that came irritated would calm
with your peaceful to and fro,
even when we couldn't solve their problems.

When we retired you sat under the arbor,
where I drank tea and watched the birds.
How many hours of music, sports radio
or baseball games did we listen to?
How many glasses of wine in the evenings?

Through all those years you didn't once complain.
But time, and weather, and my weight took its toll.
One day there was a loud crack,
and we leaned sharply to port.

I propped you against a post,
and sat next to you – it wasn't the same.
Still if it had been left up to me
you would still be there.

Fluttering Thoughts

Watching a butterfly go from flower to flower,
I wonder if it has a plan or is each visit random.
How does it choose the next flower?
Is it color, or shape, or scent?

Probably all three, but scent enticed it here.
Like the pheromones of the female attract the males downwind.
Like a woman's perfume leaves a scented trail
that turns heads at a party.

Scents bring forth memories and feelings of long ago.
As the perfume I place along the edge of my pillow,
so, at night when the lights are out, I lay down,
take a deep breath and pretend you are here.

A Different You, A Different Me

I was handed a picture of a man unknown to me.
Who is he? What is he like? What can we tell?
Does a picture show us much?

He seems pleasant enough. Maybe 30 or 40.
Clean shaven. Blue dress shirt; open at the neck.
Sleeves rolled up to his elbows.
A thoughtful expression on his face.

Is he thoughtful? Kind? Generous?
If I was introduced to him would I know more?
Not really. Maybe his name. Where he lives.
I might walk away knowing no more than I know now.

It was William James that suggested
we have as many personalities as the people we meet
and the image of us they take away with them.
We are many 'persons' to those with whom we interact.

My wife and daughters know me best,
yet they would describe me differently.
My colleagues know me on a different level,
while my former students on another.
Close friends might have a better idea
than an acquaintance at the neighborhood bar.

Am I the same person *here* as I am *there*?
Do I slightly modify my behavior to the group I'm with?
Is there a *real me*? Or am I an ensemble of *possible mes*?

Interesting isn't it?
Each of us generally the same person,
but slightly different to one another.
A slightly different me. A slightly different you.

The Old One

I've stood here so long,
a hundred years or more,
and been such a presence
few pay me any attention.

To get here I admit to being
self-centered; pushing myself upward.
When I found an opening,
I didn't hesitate. I seized it.

No looking back for me.
If others tumbled or succumbed,
well that's the nature of things isn't it?
Don't be shocked. You've done the same.

Those in my shadow are waiting
for me to stumble.
Just like I waited all those years ago.
Soon my age, disease or accident
will provide an opening.

From a little acorn, a mighty oak will grow.

Windmill

Early morning, the birds sing at the break of day,
as I sit behind the family farm house
sipping a cup of tea.
Beyond the patio at the edge of the field
an old windmill stands –
a sentry of a time passed and almost forgotten.

As the sky brightens,
the singing of the birds increases,
a cow bellows in a faraway field,
the wind freshens,
and the windmill's blades begin to turn.

Slowly they gain speed and begin to sing,
as the legs and joints squeaked in harmony,
a song of days gone by –

"Remember the days I filled the trough
that cattle visited in the morning and at night?
Or on a hot summer day when children
skinny-dipped to cool and play?
When the family listened to my songs?
Now those days are gone,
but do you remember those days long gone by?"

Yes. Yes, I remember.

Crossing the Desert

The ribbon of two-lane road
cut through the dry, barren landscape,
narrowed into the distance
and vanished on the horizon.

Ominous gray clouds pressed against the road.
The top of the car seemed to scrape against them,
as we drove mile after depressing mile,
with nothing but rocks and sand
extending in all directions.

Gloom settled itself among us;
the only sound –
the monotonous hum of the tires on the pavement.

Finally. A road sign –
Psychotic Breakdown, 110 miles.

Random Thoughts on a Ribbon Road

Leaving my daughter's home
in a small town almost on the Texas border,
instead of turning right to catch the highway,
I turned left taking the long way home.

A two-lane road of small towns,
poor cell phone connection,
no radio; just the sound of tires
on a blacktop road that looks like
a patch-work quilt in places.

Passing through the town of Rubottom,
consisting of a few houses and a Baptist Church,
the pickup truck in front of me
turns off heading home.

For the rest of the trip,
I will have the right lane to myself.
Only two cars and a truck passed me on the left
as I made my way to Ryan.

But the road – what a wonderful road.
Long and narrow stretching out in front of me,
disappearing in the distance behind me.
And in some places the horizon is in view
all around me.

A turtle crossing the road in the left lane
ignores me as it ambles on its way.
All the rain has filled the creeks and ponds
causing a case of wanderlust.
Its only predator to avoid has four wheels.

Later I see a turtle, tortoise, and tarantula
in the right lane, but they are easily avoided.
Which makes me wonder,
"How can I see a tarantula at 70 mph,
and not see my car keys standing still?"

The rain has made the vegetation lush.
One low area is a thick stand of narrow-leaf cattail,

complete with a red-winged black bird.
Other areas are filled with wild flowers –
daisies, Queen Ann's-lace, Russian thistle;
colors blur as I drive by.

Two buzzards are flushed from the bar ditch,
where they were probably snacking
on a tasty piece of road kill.

Passing a large meadow with seemly
hundreds of round bales,
I wondered how they managed mow the area,
dry the grass and bale it with all the rain we've had.
And then marvel at the land's productivity.

The road stretching out ahead,
meeting the pale blue sky.
Just me, the road and thought,
and a sense that I didn't want it to end.

At Ryan, stopped to make the turn North,
I hesitated. The urge is to continue West.
Maybe New Mexico – a small art
community in the mountains.
Something like Alpine in south Texas.

Envisioned a postcard,

> Sell the house.
> Bring the dogs.
> To hell with the rest.

as I turned right and headed home.

Be a Blessing

When my daughter dropped
her youngest at school
instead of saying "Be good,"
or "Do well," she would say
"Be a blessing."

Be a blessing. Be nice.
Help someone today. Smile.
Say a kind word. Listen
to your friend's worries.
Share your lunch. Be kind.
Be a Blessing.

It's not hard to do.
A smile. A compliment.
A simple hello.
It doesn't take much.
There is no expense.

Be a blessing.

ABOUT THE AUTHOR

Robert D. Williams was born in San Diego, California, at the Naval Hospital while his father was stationed there. From there he crossed an ocean and crisscrossed the United States until they settled in Wichita Falls, Texas where he finished high school and attended college. He married Pat after graduation and they left so he could attend graduate school finishing his degrees at Purdue University where he earned a doctorate in plant physiology. Robert began working for the USDA Agricultural Research Service as a research scientist in Mississippi and then transferred to Oklahoma. Daughters Sarah and Ann joined Pat and Robert along the way. Robert retired in 2011 to become a senior citizen with time to indulge his interests in people, reading, doing pen and ink drawings, and writing. He particularly likes to journal and write at a quiet bar top. When poetry open to him through the Writer's Corner he gladly joined in writing a genre that open new avenues of expression. Now in the second half of his 70 years poetry allows him an outlet writing about topics that are funny and light hearted, as well as serious and thought provoking. In 2019 he published his first book of poetry, The Backroad and Other Poems.

Made in the USA
Coppell, TX
10 November 2020

41090705R00049